Las Vegas FUN FACTS

John Gollehon

GOLLEHON BOOKS™
GRAND RAPIDS, MICHIGAN

Copyright © 2000 by John Gollehon

ALL RIGHTS RESERVED under international and Pan-American copyright conventions.

No part of this book may be reproduced or copied in any form or by any means, including graphic, electronic, mechanical, or information and retrieval systems, without written permission of the publisher.

Newspapers or magazine writers may quote brief passages for inclusion in a feature article or review, provided full credit is given.

MANUFACTURED IN THE UNITED STATES OF AMERICA

ISBN 0-914839-55-1

(International Standard Book Number)

GOLLEHON and LAS VEGAS FUN FACTS are exclusive trademarks of Gollehon Press, Inc.

GOLLEHON BOOKS are published by: Gollehon Press, Inc., 6157 28th St. SE, Grand Rapids, MI 49546.

GOLLEHON BOOKS are available in quantity purchases; contact Special Sales. Gollehon does not accept unsolicited manuscripts. Brief book proposals are reviewed.

When you play,
play with caution,
play with patience.
You can't win
without them.

—*John Gollehon*

Enjoy All Three Gollehon Books In This Exciting New Format:

Las Vegas Fun Facts
Casino Fun Facts
A Gambler's Little Instruction Book

At casino gift shops and bookstores everywhere.

[1] There are more churches in Las Vegas, per capita, than in any other city in the United States. Over 65 religious faiths are represented in more than 500 churches. No, the churches don't have neon signs. It would seem as if the "Sin City" stigma is a bit out of touch with reality. Tourists only see the glitz and sometimes the gaudy aspects of Las Vegas, but there is a real city there just like yours, made up of hard-working people who are proud to call Las Vegas their home.

Las Vegas Fun Facts

Las Vegas Fun Facts

2 Johnny Carson never owned the Aladdin although he would have liked to, but Wayne Newton did, in the early 1980s. From its chips to its faucets, Aladdin's magic lamp is everywhere. Of all the celebrities to be married in Las Vegas, the Aladdin scored the biggest coup in 1967 with the marriage of Elvis and Priscilla. With its re-opening in 2000, the 1966-vintage Aladdin became the first Las Vegas hotel to be closed, imploded, rebuilt, and re-opened without a change in name.

3 The National Weather Service says you only have a one in 35 chance that it will rain on any given day in Las Vegas, but when thunderstorms come around, look out! Las Vegas gets the prize for having the most spectacular electrical storms. Not surprising for a city where everything else is "spectacular"! But if you've never seen the fireworks outside your guest-room window, you might, at least, have had a chance to see a real honest-to-gosh desert sandstorm. Winds have been clocked at greater than hurricane speeds, literally sand-blasting unprotected cars.

Las Vegas Fun Facts

Las Vegas Fun Facts

4 Walk into Binion's Horseshoe Club with a million bucks in a suitcase, and you can put it all on the line, so they say, and if you win, you can do it again, but you can't bet *two* million. Your first bet sets the limit. All casinos set limits, although most are in the range of two to four thousand dollars. Casinos set maximum-bet limits to protect themselves from players who use a system of simply doubling a losing wager, and continuing to do so, until the player ultimately wins.

5 Elvis Presley first played Las Vegas at the New Frontier in 1956, but, surprisingly, his show was not exactly overrun by fans. After only one week of a two-week engagement, Elvis got the boot. This great entertainer was only at the forefront of his career. It would be 13 years later when Elvis would make his "comeback" performance in 1969 at the International Hotel (renamed the Las Vegas Hilton in 1970), the first of many SRO performances to delight his fans.

Las Vegas Fun Facts

Las Vegas Fun Facts

6 Rumor has it that Howard Hughes enjoyed his stay at the Desert Inn so much that he wanted to buy the hotel. He had lived on the entire fifth floor for nearly four years. But the truth is, the hotel operators wanted him out because they needed the rooms. Hughes solved his dilemma by simply buying the hotel! He would later buy or build seven more hotels in Las Vegas, including the Landmark, the Frontier, the Silver Slipper, the Sands, and the Castaways. This eccentric mogul died in 1976 on a flight from Acapulco.

7 Most people think that the Flamingo Hotel was the brainchild of Benjamin "Bugsy" Siegel, but not so. Siegel would later team up with Meyer Lansky and Frank Costello to finish the plans of the actual founder, Billy Wilkerson, who had started the project but ran out of funds. Siegel knew what he wanted to call his hotel, he just didn't know how to spell it. The infamous mobster actually thought "them pink birds" were called "flemencos."

Las Vegas Fun Facts

Las Vegas Fun Facts

8 Las Vegas is surrounded by the Mohave Desert, which contributes greatly to Nevada's claim of being the state with the lowest annual rainfall, barely more than eight inches per year. Desert springs abound, but certainly cannot provide the water to quench one of the United States' fastest growing cities. The damming of the great Colorado River in 1931 with the creation of Boulder Dam (now Hoover Dam) continues to provide water and electrical power to Las Vegas, although the limits of both are now sorely tested.

9 If you don't like crowds, plan your Las Vegas trip between Thanksgiving and Christmas, the slowest time of the year. Another suggestion: Avoid the weekends. A better suggestion: Check out the Las Vegas Convention & Visitors Bureau Web site. Many of the biggest trade shows in the United States can only set up in Las Vegas because no other city can provide enough hotel rooms for all those who attend. Do you really want to compete with 120,000 conventioneers fighting for that same parking space you are?

Las Vegas Fun Facts

Las Vegas Fun Facts

10 In 1999, an alumni cast-member reunion enjoyed a special 40th birthday performance of Folies Bergere, the Tropicana's longest-running stage performance in Las Vegas. Entertainment Director Lou Walters, father of Barbara Walters, brought the show to Las Vegas. It was the Dunes Hotel, however, earlier in the '50s, that scored a "first" for Las Vegas when it filled its showroom stage with bare-breasted dancers. Although the Dunes opened in 1955 to modest success, it was on this day in 1957 that things really started to take off.

11 The Pioneer Club had a long and storied history in downtown Las Vegas, but its real claim to fame happened in 1947 when the "Howdy Partner" cowboy was installed atop the casino as a promotion sponsored by the Chamber of Commerce.

12 Fremont Street, the main drag in downtown Las Vegas, is named after explorer John C. Fremont, but did you know that Carson City, Nevada's capital, is named after Fremont's trusty scout, Kit Carson?

Las Vegas Fun Facts

Las Vegas Fun Facts

13 Most visitors to Las Vegas would guess that the humidity is about 10 percent, but it's actually 29 percent on average, which is still considered quite low. People with allergies or skin problems usually prefer a dry climate. And, best of all, Las Vegas does not have bugs! That's right. Not even pesky mosquitoes, thanks to the dry air and infrequent rain. There simply are no stagnant ponds for the little buggers to breed.

14 Las Vegas is also known as the Wedding Capital Of The World. Wedding chapels are everywhere! It's not unusual for nearly 3,000 weddings to take place over the Valentine's Day weekend. Weddings are popular because there's no blood-test requirement and no waiting period to think it over. It would be wise, therefore, to do this when you're sober. All you need is some form of identification, a few bucks for the marriage license, a place to tie the knot, and… oh, yeah… a minister.

Las Vegas Fun Facts

Las Vegas Fun Facts

15 A four-hour drive from Las Vegas gets you to the Grand Canyon. The air tours are great, but the mule rides are exhilarating. Pick a mule with good eyesight because the ledges they walk on around the mile-deep canyon are only a few feet wide.

16 Lake Mead is no more than 40 minutes from the Strip, the place to be on a hot July day. There's every conceivable form of water recreation available. Most visitors see Lake Mead from the air as they prepare to land, but few actually venture the short distance to enjoy it.

17 If the summer heat's getting to you, other than the heat of a hot dice table, that is… just head for Mount Charleston, only 40 minutes from the Las Vegas Strip and a good 30 degrees cooler. There's horseback riding, scenic walking trails among the tall pines, and a breathtaking view of the valley below you. In the winter, you can ski to your heart's content, while your kids enjoy a good snowball fight!

Las Vegas Fun Facts

Las Vegas Fun Facts

18 One of the Strip's top attractions for passersby, Treasure Island's Buccaneer Bay, draws crowds right off the street to watch a hearty exchange of cannon fire. The pirates always win, and the British ship goes down in 90 feet of churning water. Today, gambling in Las Vegas is all in the packaging. Hotel facades are attractions in and of themselves, but what's inside the package is all the same: If you see one casino… you've seen them all.

19 Many of those who saw Andrew Lloyd Webber's "Starlight Express" at the Las Vegas Hilton in the '90s were so impressed by the musical score that the Hilton was besieged with requests for CDs, but none were available. Eventually, sound tracks from the London performance made it to the U.S. market. The '90s decade signaled a change in entertainment in Las Vegas, from big-name acts to broadway production shows. Today, however, top-name entertainers appealing to the younger set seem to be adding to the mix.

Las Vegas Fun Facts

Las Vegas Fun Facts

20 The first "theme park" in Las Vegas was not the MGM Grand, as most people would guess. When the Last Frontier opened in 1943, the Last Frontier Village was built next door, full of shops, a miniature train ride, and "Old West" amusements. In 1998, the Frontier changed its name back to the New Frontier, as it was known from 1955 to 1967, following settlement of a long and bitter strike by the Culinary Union. Called in 1991, the strike was the longest in U.S. history.

21 Wanna party? I kinda thought so. You're in Vegas, right! So what Las Vegas hotel comes to mind when you think about "Mardi Gras" or "Carnivale"? Indeed! It's always party-time at the Rio! Opened in 1990, this beautiful hotel brought a new look to Vegas, including its Masquerade Village, opened in 1997. The Rio's popular Masquerade Show treats guests to outlandish performances several times a day. At night the hotel's miles of neon is spectacular in itself.

Las Vegas Fun Facts

Las Vegas Fun Facts

22

Sam Boyd is a story of perseverance. Starting out as a dealer in the early '40s, he parlayed his savings into a piece of the Sahara, then joined Milton Prell—who had owned the Sahara—in building downtown's Mint in 1957. Next on his list was Union Plaza in 1971, sporting the world's largest casino at the time. He cleaned up the Stardust Hotel in 1985, and went on to build Sam's Town, one of Las Vegas' most popular hotels, particularly among the locals.

23 The $800 million Paris Las Vegas resort's signature is most definitely the 50-story-tall replica of the Eiffel Tower. The original is 984 feet tall. Visitors can also enjoy the Arc de Triomphe, Champs Elysee, the Paris Opera House, Parc Monceau, and—believe it—the River Seine.

24 The Hard Rock Hotel & Casino in Las Vegas is really into "saving the planet" by recycling all glass, metal, and paper products used on site. The big "guitar" marquee is the draw on the outside, but inside, Elton John's flashy piano would put Liberace to shame.

Las Vegas Fun Facts

Las Vegas Fun Facts

25 Palace Station has one of the biggest signs in Las Vegas. It has to. It's not on the Strip; it's not downtown. It's not even on Boulder Highway. It's on Sahara Avenue, which means that famous sign has a big job to do in luring travelers off I-15. But the Palace Station draws plenty of local customers, going back to the days when it was known as the Bingo Palace. Many of the lowest table-minimum bets in town are posted at the "Palace."

26 Mandalay Bay is unique in the sense that it "shares" its property with the famous Four Seasons Hotel, Las Vegas' first Five Diamond award winner. For those staying at the Four Seasons, guests enjoy a private entrance, parking, and check-in. Mandalay Bay features a "wave pool," complete with white sand beaches and tropical plants. Built in 1999, this is truly the place to go if you want to be pampered.

Las Vegas Fun Facts

Las Vegas Fun Facts

27 Liberace opened the Riviera Hotel in April of 1955, getting a then-unheard-of $50,000 a week! It was the ninth major resort on the bustling Strip, standing tall over all the others at a whopping nine stories! A year later, the new 15-story Fremont Hotel in downtown Las Vegas would become Nevada's tallest building. The early '50s marked the end of the bungalow-type resorts, favored by Hollywood stars accustomed to that cozy, ranch-like ambiance. Now, with the price of land soaring, the race to build was upward.

28 When it opened in 1957 the Tropicana Hotel became the most expensive resort built in Las Vegas. It cost over $15 million, and that didn't include the cost of a 60-foot-tall tulip-shaped fountain in front of the hotel, pegged at a cool hundred grand. Its 1985 remodeling gave the "Trop" a tropical theme, complete with parrots and lush plants scattered throughout a five-acre water park that featured "swim-up" blackjack tables. That's right. Swimsuits were the proper attire.

Las Vegas Fun Facts

Las Vegas Fun Facts

29 Legendary casino owner, Tony Cornero, was the force behind the Stardust Hotel. Started in 1954, it took four years to complete. He made his name by operating three gambling ships that sailed out of San Diego in the '30s and '40s. Incidentally, gambling chips from the S.S. Rex, S.S. Tango, and S.S. Lux are now highly collectible. Cornero, unfortunately, never got to see his Strip hotel open. He died with his boots on, shooting craps at the Desert Inn in 1955.

30 A popular tourist attraction skirting the Nevada/California border is Death Valley, the lowest point in the United States at 282 feet below sea level. The hottest temperatures are routinely recorded there in the summer, although winter daytime temperatures might only be in the 50s. Las Vegas is blessed with nearby tourist attractions, including Zion and Bryce Canyon National Parks in Utah. Closer to Las Vegas, Red Rock Canyon is a must-see for weary-eyed gamblers who need a break from the action.

Las Vegas Fun Facts

Las Vegas Fun Facts

31 The opening performance of "Hallelujah Hollywood" marked an otherwise slow 1974 in Las Vegas. The hottest tickets in town were ringside seats for this showgirl spectacular in the original MGM Grand's Ziegfeld Room. With Dean Martin in the Celebrity Room, not to mention the world's largest casino (at the time) jammed to the hilt, this one-year-old behemoth on the Strip was THE place to be.

32 Besides being the first casino-resort on what is now the Las Vegas Strip, the El Rancho Vegas also claimed to be the first Las Vegas hotel to offer buffets. The cost: one dollar. The Mint downtown claims it was the first to offer that other Las Vegas tradition… the 50-cent shrimp cocktail. And the Union Plaza downtown says in its press release that it was "…the first to offer women dealers." So how many do you want?

Las Vegas Fun Facts

Las Vegas Fun Facts

33 As you might imagine, casinos have the most elaborate security systems in the world. Sensitive cameras can zoom in and read the date on a quarter, just before it's fed to a hungry slot machine. And those cameras are one of the reasons why your own personal camera is not allowed in casinos. A flash could knock out the surveillance equipment. Another reason cameras are taboo in casinos is to protect everyone's privacy. No one wants to be in someone else's family album.

34 An attraction that many visitors are not aware of is ghost towns. Nevada is full of them, and there's at least three within driving distance of Las Vegas. You want to go see one? I don't know where they are, but ask a bellman. If you're bored with the games, or the convention you're supposed to be attending, and you want to go out in the desert by yourself, like an idiot, and get lost, that's your business.

Las Vegas Fun Facts

Las Vegas Fun Facts

35 Las Vegas has some really incredible rain storms that can drench the city in a matter of hours. Some of the worst floods have stacked up cars and literally moved buildings. When there's a flood warning, and you see water rushing into the casino, most sensible players get out. But not slot players, apparently. They just stay there playing in five inches of water! Someone has to remind these diehards that slot machines are electrical!

36 If you're heading for Hoover Dam, you'll probably pass through Boulder City, a quaint town with a most interesting point of trivia: Boulder City is the only town in Nevada where gambling is *not* legal! The town was essentially built in 1931 to house the men working on Hoover Dam, an absolute marvel of engineering. Plan on spending a considerable part of your day for this fascinating excursion. Another point of trivia, albeit a chilling one: The first and the last to die in the building of Hoover Dam were father and son.

Las Vegas Fun Facts

Las Vegas Fun Facts

37 Howard Hughes certainly left his mark on Las Vegas, parlaying well over half a billion dollars from the sale of his TWA stock. And, as you might expect, he left a few bucks when he died. His estate was contested for years, and several wills were presented to the courts, but all were declared bogus. Estimates on the value of his estate vary, but it is believed that nearly $7 billion was split up among two dozen *distant* relatives.

38 If someone were to ask you how much money Las Vegas casinos make every year from slot machines, you probably wouldn't know, would you? But you would admit, wouldn't you, that some of it is yours?! Here's a fact that's hard to believe: Almost 60 percent of all the casino profits comes from slot machines! Hey, they're not called "One-Armed Bandits" for nothing! Take my advice: Learn blackjack!

Las Vegas Fun Facts

Las Vegas Fun Facts

39 When you're at the Mirage, be sure to visit the 2.5 million-gallon Dolphin Habitat, the largest saltwater pool in the world. The Atlantic bottlenose dolphins that romp and play with each other are a treat to watch, but they cannot survive in fresh water. The Mirage is quick to point out that none of the dolphins were taken from the wild. While there, look for Siegfried & Roy's exotic animals—many are used in the show. Although the white tigers are kept in their own special habitat, many of the animals are kept in the "Secret Garden." See if you can find it.

40 Jay Sarno built two of Las Vegas' most eye-catching hotels: Caesars Palace in 1966 and Circus Circus in 1968. Although modestly successful at the outset, it wasn't until William Bennet took over in 1974 that Circus Circus began its corporate climb. Sarno, however, was happy just being a designer. If you look closely at the cement latticework that completely encases Caesars Palace, through which that eerie blue-green light emanates, you'll see that the design is made up of cast-cement blocks in the shape of a square "S." So now we know that Sarno had at least a touch of ego.

Las Vegas Fun Facts

Las Vegas Fun Facts

41 Rent a copy of the 1960 Frank Sinatra film, *Ocean's 11*. Believe it or not, the premise was to blow up the electrical towers feeding power to Las Vegas. When all the lights would go out, and before backup power could be generated, the "rat pack" would clean out the vaults of the Sahara, Sands, Riviera, Desert Inn, and Flamingo hotels. The movie was set during the holidays but was filmed during the summer. While the movie was being shot, summer vacationers to Las Vegas were wondering why there were Christmas decorations all over town.

42 Although the railroads brought plenty of workers to Las Vegas in 1904, it was the construction of Boulder Dam (now Hoover Dam) that put Las Vegas on the map. The year was 1931, during the Great Depression, when literally thousands of unemployed men journeyed to this whistle-stop in the desert, only to be turned away because the jobs were already taken. During that same year, gambling became legalized in Nevada, and, although not exactly a "notable event," divorce laws were relaxed. You could lose your money, and your honey, at the same time.

Las Vegas Fun Facts

Las Vegas Fun Facts

43 In the 1930s, Las Vegas was just about the only place left to experience the last of the frontier towns, where you could walk down Fremont Street complete with bordellos and saloons and general stores, and more hitching posts that parking spots. There was a "Wild West" ambiance to the street, but it was fading fast. Fremont Street would become Glitter Gulch by the '50s, Casino Center by the '70s, and the Fremont Street Experience by the '90s. And not a hitching post in sight.

44 A fire raced through the original MGM Grand Hotel (now Bally's) early in the morning of November 21, 1980, claiming 85 lives. The enormous casino was completely gutted in seconds. The MGM Grand was named after the 1932 movie, *Grand Hotel*. For many years after its gala opening in 1973, it would seem as if Dean Martin's name was always on the marquee, playing the room he opened, the famous Celebrity Room.

Las Vegas Fun Facts

Las Vegas Fun Facts

45 World War II would usher in new military installations including a strategic air field north of Las Vegas, later to be named Nellis Air Force Base. Even while the war was going on, Las Vegas continued to earn a deserving reputation for top entertainment. No one could hold a candle (even a candelabra) to Mr. Entertainment. That's right: Liberace. And Sammy Davis Jr., was making inroads for his career, if not for civil rights causes, which would come later. The great Candy Man himself had to enter and leave hotels in the back, through the kitchen.

46 Most people would say that the first hotel/casino to be built on what would become the Las Vegas Strip was the Flamingo, but that's not even close. The very first resort was the El Rancho Vegas. There were several "clubs" on the road before the El Rancho Vegas was built in 1941, but that's all they were, more like bars, not plush resorts. The famed El Rancho Vegas was located directly across the Strip from the present-day Sahara Hotel.

Las Vegas Fun Facts

Las Vegas Fun Facts

47 Before the Las Vegas Strip got its name, it was simply known as the Los Angeles Highway. And for good reason: It led straight to Los Angeles! It was also known as U.S. 91, which is what the locals called it when it was just a dusty road with a motel and a club here and there. Perhaps the most popular club on the road was the Club Bingo, which would later become part of the Sahara Hotel in 1952. The 91 Club, another popular watering-hole, stood where the Last Frontier would be built in 1943, becoming the Strip's second major hotel/casino.

48 The Las Vegas Strip would welcome Bugsy Siegel's Flamingo in 1946, and the Thunderbird Hotel would be built in 1948, ending the decade with four plush casino resorts. Construction continued throughout the '50s, beginning with the Desert Inn in 1950, the Sahara and the Sands in 1952, the Dunes and the Riviera in 1955, the Hacienda in 1956, the Tropicana in 1957, and the Stardust in 1958. The Aladdin and Caesars Palace would open in 1966, ending a nearly nine-year lapse in hotel construction.

Las Vegas Fun Facts

Las Vegas Fun Facts

49 Most newcomers to Las Vegas get "turned around" as they walk or drive the Strip. And it's easy to see why. The Strip makes a fairly sharp bend near the Venetian which few visitors realize. The intersection of the Strip and Flamingo Road, where Bally's is located, makes perfect compass points. Bally's is on the southeast of the corner, the Bellagio is on the southwest, Caesars Palace is on the northwest, and Barbary Coast is on the northeast. This famous corner used to be the busiest in the world, but today that title has shifted south to the corner of the Strip and Tropicana Blvd.

50 The Luxor is one of Las Vegas' most intriguing hotels. A powerful beam of light emanates over ten miles into the night sky from the top of a giant pyramid. Jet pilots claim they can see the Luxor's beam on a clear evening as far away as Los Angeles. The name *Luxor* refers to Al Uqsur, Egypt's most exotic tourist locale, on the banks of the Nile. The Luxor's dramatic re-creation of the Sphinx, with the body of a lion and the head of a man, leaves guests awestruck as they enter the pyramid.

Las Vegas Fun Facts

Las Vegas Fun Facts

51 The name *Las Vegas* means "The Meadows" in Spanish. In fact, the valley was an oasis in the desert, providing spring water for the Anasazi Indians, who first inhabited the area. The Anasazi tribe was forced out of the valley more than a thousand years ago by the Paiute Indians. The name *Nevada*, incidentally, means "Snowcapped." Las Vegas is situated in the southern tip of the state, only four or five hours by car from its principal player market, Southern California.

52 If you were at the Las Vegas Hilton during 1992, you might have watched the filming for the blockbuster 1993 movie, *Indecent Proposal*, starring Robert Redford, Demi Moore, and Woody Harrelson. Jack Engelhard wrote the novel. The 1971 film, *Diamonds Are Forever*, also featured casino interiors of the Hilton, not to mention a "high wire" act atop the hotel. Shirley Bassey returned to do the title song. The hotel was called "The White House" in the Sean Connery film.

Las Vegas Fun Facts

Las Vegas Fun Facts

53 Here's a misleading statistic for you, cheerfully provided by the Las Vegas Chamber of Commerce: The average temperature in Las Vegas is a comfortable 66.3 degrees. Excuse me?! If you visit Las Vegas in the summer, when temperatures can exceed 110 degrees for days on end, you'll think these marketing wizards have been out in the sun too long. Well, thanks to its relatively cool winters, Las Vegas does have a nice average temperature. Oh, and another thing. When it's hot, really hot, it's not really that hot because the humidity is low. Right.

54 It took a while to build, but when the Desert Inn finally opened on April 24, 1950, everyone was talking about the hotel's rather bizarre color scheme: Everything was decked out in Bermuda pink and emerald green, including the blackjack tables! Edgar Bergen and Charlie McCarthy opened the Painted Desert Showroom (pink and green, I imagine). The "DI" had the first 18-hole golf course in Las Vegas, bringing such notables as Sam Snead and Gene Littler to its tournaments. That's right… the fairways were green, the flags were pink.

Las Vegas Fun Facts

Las Vegas Fun Facts

55 During the '50s, Las Vegas Strip hotels had this thing about slogans. The Sands was dubbed "A Place In The Sun." The Last Frontier was "The Early West In Modern Splendor." The Sahara was known as "The Jewel In The Desert." The Tropicana was called "The Tiffany Of The Strip." The Thunderbird was known as "The Sacred Bearer Of Happiness Unlimited," in honor of the Navajo legend of the Thunderbird, I guess. Today, only the original Sahara and Tropicana still stand. I guess they had the best slogans.

56 In 1951, Benny Binion bought the Eldorado Club, a "sawdust joint" in the old Apache Hotel, renamed it The Horseshoe Club, and refurbished it with wall-to-wall carpeting. The spanky new resorts on the Strip had plush carpet everywhere, but downtown casinos still looked like saloons. Well, after the "colorful" gray-and-brown carpet was laid, the Horseshoe Club had an unforeseen problem: "We had to tell our customers not to squash out their cigarettes on the floor," said Binion. Soon after, Binion placed an order for two thousand more ashtrays.

Las Vegas Fun Facts

Las Vegas Fun Facts

57 The Apache Hotel opened downtown in 1932 with a new contraption: an elevator. Gosh knows it needed it; the hotel was all of three stories. Nearby, the Northern Club was already operating a casino, the first to be licensed in Las Vegas. But the Boulder Club, the oldest on Fremont Street, was already offering a game or two when it opened in 1929, two years before legalized gambling. It got square with the State in 1931, receiving the second gaming license issued in the county.

58 The 1995 movie, *Casino*, rekindled the image of a criminal element in Las Vegas, at a time when the gaming mecca was just beginning to shake that troubling stigma. Corporations control Las Vegas today, legitimate, publicly-traded companies. Running a casino today is not much different from running any other kind of business. But in the Hollywood version, who could forget Joe Pesci as the stereotyped Nicky. The trilogy was the treat of Martin Scorsese, whose other related films were *Mean Streets* and *GoodFellas*.

Las Vegas Fun Facts

Las Vegas Fun Facts

59 One of the most famous trademarks, the MGM lion, a 100,000-pound bronze statue, welcomes guests to the MGM Grand hotel. The lion, named Metro, incidentally, is 45 feet tall, sitting atop a 25-foot pedestal. The hotel is lit at night in an extraordinary blaze of color and technology. It was Barbra Streisand who helped Las Vegas welcome in the new millennium at the Grand Garden Arena, home to major concerts and sporting events.

60 Old-timers still call downtown Las Vegas "Glitter Gulch," but it's been promoted since 1995 as the Fremont Street Experience. It's a huge, 90-feet-high canopy covered in over two million lights all controlled by a computer that produces dazzling images. It also produces high-energy music in sync with the sights that can make the bones in your ears vibrate. If you want to see (and hear) the "new" downtown, bring your money, your walking shoes, and your earplugs.

Las Vegas Fun Facts

Las Vegas Fun Facts

61 Yes, it has sauerkraut and mustard, and you can get it from a sidewalk cart at New York-New York, the tallest hotel in Nevada at the time of its construction. You can't miss the Empire State Building towering over all the others at 529 feet... that's 47 stories! It even has a replica of the Brooklyn Bridge, and this is no slouch, either. It's 300 feet long! Rumor has it that cab drivers even become rude when they turn in to the hotel.

62 During the early '60s, years of construction at the northwest corner of the Strip and Flamingo Road gave no clue of what was about to rise from the desert. No one even knew its name. Newspapers weren't even sure what to call it. Call it Caesars Palace, and call it palatial. Its showroom may very well have the most recognized name: Circus Maximus, opened by Andy Williams who didn't waste any time getting to his signature song, *Moon River*. Brothers Stuart and Clifford Perlman owned the hotel for many years, parlaying a string of hot dog stands into one of the world's most famous hotels.

Las Vegas Fun Facts

Las Vegas Fun Facts

63

The place was Caesars Palace; blackjack was the game. Dustin Hoffman played an autistic savant who beat the game by counting the cards. Tom Cruise played the role of his younger brother. Who doesn't remember *Rain Man*, the award-winning 1988 film? But like all movies, there's a reality problem here that needs to be sorted out. Card-counting was the hit of the '60s. It actually caught casinos by surprise! Today, however, and even in 1988, Las Vegas casino bosses would never let their money scoot out the door quite that easily. Only in Hollywood.

64 Opened in 1954 as the Desert Showboat Motor Inn, believe it or not, the Showboat is a popular stop for locals, not to mention professional bowlers, who compete every year in one of the P.B.A. tour's top events. It's one of the country's largest facilities with over 100 lanes. Besides bowling, the Showboat climbed in popularity with its 1,500 seat bingo parlor and fabulous buffets. Today, the locals love it because it's a "Strip quality" casino *off* the Strip. Translation: Away from the traffic!

Las Vegas Fun Facts

Las Vegas Fun Facts

65 Can you name the all-time top entertainer in Las Vegas? Neil Diamond was a smash in his debut at the Aladdin in 1976, and what about talk-show legend Johnny Carson, a showroom favorite of the Sahara in the '60s and '70s? Diana Ross, Tom Jones, Elvis, Paul Anka, Wayne Newton, Barbra Streisand? It's a tough call. But if you ask the casino executives who they would list on top, the answer is a clear choice: Whether it was Caesars Palace, the Sands, or the Desert Inn, they knew they had a casino full of high rollers when Frank Sinatra's name was on the marquee!

66 The producers of the action-movie *Con Air* filmed the implosion of the Sands Hotel tower in 1996, and later edited the scene into the movie as part of a spectacular plane crash on the Las Vegas Strip. The ringleader of the escape was played by John Malkovich. The star of the film was Nicolas Cage. The demise of the Sands, particularly as it was exploited in this movie, was hardly a fitting tribute to its memory.

Las Vegas Fun Facts

Las Vegas Fun Facts

67 Do you know what famous-name casino opened on the Strip in 1968 *without* a hotel? I'll give you a hint: It's pink and white, and the hotel came four years later. That's right. Circus Circus is a *real* circus with a carnival midway under the big top. There's one in Reno, too. But this property is not all games for the kids (not to mention adults). One of its restaurants, called "The Steak House," has beaten out Chicago, New York, and Kansas City's prime. Make mine medium.

68 In 1956, Las Vegas experienced its first "room glut," the lowest room occupancy rate in its history. The owners of the new Hacienda, at the far south end of the Strip, didn't care, however, expecting their new hotel to be the first stop for travelers from Southern California. It was, until they found out the casino wasn't open! The Gaming Control Board kept the casino closed for over a year.

Las Vegas Fun Facts

Las Vegas Fun Facts

69 Well before this mega-resort was to be built, someone came up with the idea of staging a contest to "Name The Castle." The lucky winner was awarded $25,000, and the resort-to-be was officially dubbed "Excalibur" on September 28th, 1988, two years before its 1990 grand opening. The gist of the legend, incidentally, is that "Excalibur," a beautiful sword embedded in stone, was pulled out by a young nobleman named Arthur, earning him the throne of England.

70 Where would you expect to see the single largest nugget of gold in the world on display? In Las Vegas? Absolutely. Which casino? Well, duh. The nugget is at the Golden Nugget, where else? And don't think you're going to walk right in and heist this thing. The "Hand Of Faith," as it's called, weighs 62 pounds. Your guess is as good as mine how much the armed guard weighs.

Las Vegas Fun Facts

Las Vegas Fun Facts

71 If you were fortunate enough to watch the Rat Pack in action at the old Sands Hotel, you're one up on the rest of us. Great memories, indeed. No matter how pretentious, how big, or how expensive, the Venetian Hotel should know that it's sitting on sacred ground. The Sands Hotel defined an era in Las Vegas that I hope you were fortunate enough to witness. It was the place where Frank Sinatra, Sammy Davis, Jr., Peter Lawford, Dean Martin, and Joey Bishop entertained in the Copa Room and the lounge, no less, like Vegas will never know again.

72 When David meets Goliath in Las Vegas, the big guy always wins. So it goes for small casinos such as the Castaways, sitting square in the path of bulldozers clearing the way for the Mirage. The Silver Slipper didn't fare much better: It was traded in for a parking lot needed by the Frontier. And the Bonanza, a little 160-room hotel, had unknowingly been built beyond its own property lines. But after a court battle, Kirk Kerkorian got that property and all the land he needed to erect his giant-sized MGM Grand Hotel (now Bally's).

Las Vegas Fun Facts

Las Vegas Fun Facts

73 Howard Hughes bought the Landmark Hotel in 1968 while it was under construction, so we can't blame him for this strange-looking contraption. The big question is, how many three-martini lunches did the architects have while designing this thing? In all fairness, it probably had more "modern" appeal in those days, looking like something the Jetsons would fly around in, but it never really got off the ground. Hughes wife, actress Jean Peters, took title to this "white elephant" as a result of her divorce settlement. Opened in 1969, it closed in 1991, and was destroyed in 1995.

74 A Las Vegas attraction you probably *don't* want to see is the underground testing of atomic bombs. The Nevada Test Site, about 65 miles northwest of Las Vegas, created its first "mushroom" in 1951. Until 1962, all the tests were done in the atmosphere. Kaboom! And you thought the Mirage's volcano was something! Las Vegas put a stop to these above-ground tests after Aunt Millie's meatloaf started to glow. Since then, all tests—and there have been over 500 of them—are done underground.

Las Vegas Fun Facts

Las Vegas Fun Facts

75 The MGM Grand is one of the largest hotels in the world. Now how many elevators would you expect a hotel like this to have? Try 93! With all those elevators, you would think there's always one sitting at the ground floor just waiting to take you to your room. Nope. You have to push that little square button at least three times, after everyone else has pushed it, and only then will an elevator door open at the farthest end away from you, where everyone else is standing.

76 Many Las Vegas visitors today can remember the old Castaways Hotel & Casino, although most would remember only the casino… the hotel was rather inconspicuous. But few visitors today would remember the Sans Souci, which is what the Castaways was known as when it opened in 1958. The Castaways had a legendary sports book run by Sonny Reizner, who would set the standard for race and sports books to come.

Las Vegas Fun Facts

Las Vegas Fun Facts

77 In 1931, the year that gaming was legalized in Nevada, the Meadows would become the first true casino/hotel when it opened on Boulder Highway. But it would be ten years later when the El Rancho Vegas opened on the Los Angeles Highway that a "destination" resort attracting visitors from Southern California would set the pace for things to come. The Meadows had a short run, but the El Rancho Vegas survived until 1960 when a mysterious fire returned it to its sand and sagebrush beginnings. It was never rebuilt.

78 The '90s in Las Vegas witnessed an unusual change in a typical casino's floor-plan. At first, more and more blackjack tables were removed to make way for more slot machines. In fact, slot machines had taken over what used to be lounges and bars and even restaurants. Casino executives quickly realized that slots could produce more profit per square foot of gaming space than any other game.

Las Vegas Fun Facts

Las Vegas Fun Facts

79

The '90s in Las Vegas also ushered in a surprising change in the choices players were making as to the games they wanted to play. The biggest surprise to gaming operators was the flattening out of interest in blackjack, a game that had made its mark in the late '60s with the introduction of "card-counting." But casino countermeasures over the years had toughened the game so much that newcomers were getting the message: The game *used* to be good.

80 Today, the table game that beckons most new players is craps. How could they miss the excitement? Everyone at the dice tables seems to be having all the fun! Now, craps has really caught on. Once players realized how simple the game is, and how low some of the bets are percentage-wise, it was an obvious choice. Now, Las Vegas casinos are installing more dice tables. As an old-time casino manager explains it, "It only took a few hundred years for the game to catch on."

Las Vegas Fun Facts

Las Vegas Fun Facts

81 Las Vegas is said to have more cellular phones per capita than any other city in the United States. It seems as if everyone has a phone stuck to their ear. "Uh, Bob, this is Harry. I've got a 16, the dealer's showing a 6. I forgot, do I hit it or stand?"

82 A hundred-dollar bill is the standard monetary unit in Las Vegas. People buy Big Macs with a "bill" and buy cars with a suitcase full of them. For some people, a "bill" is a tip. For high-rolling slot players, it's one pull. For the rest of us, it's one hundred dollars.

83 Have you ever tried to describe a Las Vegas hotel to someone who has never been there? You can probably get away with a few, but don't try it with the Venetian. If a picture is worth a thousand words, the Venetian has a thousand pictures. The incredible replica of St. Mark's Square is overwhelming. The canals of Venice are a romantic dream. It is an all-suite hotel for connoisseurs of life's *largest* pleasures.

Las Vegas Fun Facts

Las Vegas Fun Facts

84 Although it doesn't happen very often, Las Vegas blackjack bosses can exclude card-counters; they can ask them to leave the game, but they can't make them leave the casino (unless the person is unruly). Many players seem confused about this. They might be thinking about the rules and regs in Atlantic City, and other new gaming venues, where card-counters must be permitted to play, but under some rather tough playing conditions. Vegas takes a different approach.

85 The Stratosphere Tower is 1,149 feet high. You can't miss it; you can see it from everywhere. Well, someone had the brilliant idea of building a roller coaster on the very top of it called "High Roller." Cute, huh? And as if that's not enough, there's another ride called the "Big Shot," which shoots you straight up in the air while your stomach rides about ten feet below you. And speaking of your stomach, there's a revolving restaurant up there, too. In fact, there's at least a couple of places to eat. Heed my advice: Eat *after* you ride these things.

Las Vegas Fun Facts

Las Vegas Fun Facts

86 Since each floor of the Luxor Hotel is stepped inward as the pyramid rises, it's fun getting to your guest room. The elevators do not go straight up; they rise at a rather steep 29 degree angle. Of course, they are not called elevators; they are *inclinators*. When the Luxor was giving these neat rides through ancient Egyptian tombs, there were ancient coins scattered everywhere. These coins, of course, were just replicas. But in the gift shop, after the tour, visitors could buy real ones! That's right, 5,000-year-old coins were for sale! I think I'd rather take a tour of the gift shop!

87 Few Las Vegas visitors have ever heard of the Moulin Rouge Hotel & Casino, built away from the Strip in 1955, at a time when black entertainers, as well as black guests, were not welcome at other hotels. It had its ups and downs when it opened. But when Joe Louis, the late heavyweight champion of the world, became an owner of the hotel, it looked promising. After putting his heart and soul into the business, even the "Brown Bomber" couldn't make it last the 12 rounds. The Moulin Rouge finally went down for the count. The property was declared a national historic site in 1992.

Las Vegas Fun Facts

Las Vegas Fun Facts

88 Throughout the '60s and '70s, everyone's favorite Las Vegas sign was the Golden Nugget, the most photographed sign in Las Vegas. So what do you do when you have such a famous Vegas icon sitting on top of your casino? Why, if you're Steve Wynn, you take it down. It was a bold move in 1984 that didn't sit well with Vegas nostalgia buffs, or even with some city leaders. But to remodel the Golden Nugget into downtown's most lavish casino, the sign just had to go.

89 On the Strip, picking your favorite sign isn't as easy. How about the Riviera or the Flamingo Hilton, and what about the Rio just off the Strip? For many years, the Sahara boasted of having the world's tallest, free-standing sign. It should be; it's 23 stories high! The Rio is said to have the most neon, but the Stardust is in the running, too. It definitely has the most animation, with 26 different lighting sequences, which makes it tough to take its picture! It just won't stand still! Lucky The Clown at Circus Circus wins the heavyweight division, weighing in at 120 tons, the heaviest sign in town.

Las Vegas Fun Facts

Las Vegas Fun Facts

90 During the '80s, a trend was underway to use more incandescent bulbs to light up the signs, and the effect was startling. You can still see many of them today. There are literally millions of bulbs. They flash, they change color, and… they burn out. And that was the problem. The signs didn't look so hot when a few hundred out of a few thousand checked out early. How would you like to be the guy who has to change all those bulbs on a sign 70 feet up in the air? Today, bulbs are out. Neon is in. It lasts forever and a day.

91 The TV show "Vega$" showcased the Desert Inn's $50 million renovation in 1979. The series premiered in 1978, but really took off when ace-detective Dan Tanna started getting all these calls on his car-phone (pretty hip for 1979) from Bea, his secretary— best described as every guy's dream for the reception desk—telling him to meet so-and-so at the DI. But the real star of the show was that red '57 T-bird with the personal license plate that read: TANNA.

Las Vegas Fun Facts

Las Vegas Fun Facts

92 The glory days of Vegas still live in the movies with priceless scenes inside the casinos and on the Strip. Jane Russell and Victor Mature starred in *The Las Vegas Story* in 1952. Dan Dailey and Cyd Charisse were the stars in MGM's great musical, *Meet Me In Las Vegas*. But the best casino interiors are found in *Ocean's 11*. It's the Rat Pack in action, concocting a scheme to knock off five of the major casinos. Can they pull it off? The movie, filmed in 1960, can still hold your attention, though there might be a chuckle here and there.

93 The builders of Paris Las Vegas managed to bring over everything that is Paris… except the attitude. All the major landmarks are re-created in impeccable detail, highlighted by the 50-story Eiffel Tower where you can travel on a glass elevator to an observation deck for a breathtaking view of the Las Vegas Valley. On the way down, there's a little, out-of-the-way French restaurant that the *real* Paris doesn't have. Paris Las Vegas is connected to Bally's by a quaint street lined with shops that sell some of the most expensive stuff you've ever seen in your life!

Las Vegas Fun Facts

Las Vegas Fun Facts

94 A Caesars Palace press release says that the Brahma Shrine, built near the center Strip entrance to the hotel, is an "authentic replica" of Thailand's most popular Buddhist shrine. Is that an oxymoron, or what? And get this: The original Brahma Shrine was installed to ward off bad luck. Now I ask you: Does Caesars Palace really want this thing at the front of its hotel, where all the players enter on their way in to test their luck?! If that thing really works, Caesars may have to invest in black cats!

95 Who can forget the build-up to Evel Knievel's death-defying jump over the towering row of fountains at Caesars Palace? It happened on December 31, 1967, a date Knievel would probably like to forget. But on April 14, 1989, in front of a national television audience and 50,000 excited fans gathered at the hotel, Evel's son, Robbie, avenged his father's failure by performing a flawless jump into stardom, not to mention *Las Vegas Fun Facts*.

Las Vegas Fun Facts

Here's how to get your own set of John Gollehon's personal Strategy Cards and save MONEY doing it!

The author's popular Strategy Cards have become the hottest cards on the market! The set retails for $12 in shops, but you can order the complete set by mail for only $9.95. Your cards go out within 48 hours and we pay the first-class postage!

BLACKJACK: Every player-hand and dealer up-card combination is listed, so you'll know exactly when to hit, stand, split, or double down. The Strategy Card does all the work!

CRAPS: All the payoffs for the bets you'll be making are listed so you can be sure you're getting all the winnings you deserve! A complete rundown for playing the game is also included.

VIDEO POKER: Follow a clever strategy to increase your chances of hitting a royal flush by 20 percent! The best paytables are listed, so you'll know exactly what machines to look for.

ROULETTE: A precise layout of the wheel is shown so that you can clock the dealer and predict the segment where the ball should land. See if you can beat the wheel with skill!

HOW TO ORDER:

Send check or money order for only $9.95 to: Gollehon Press, Inc., 6157 28th St. SE, Grand Rapids, MI 49546. Just write "Strategy Cards" on a piece of paper along with your name and address printed neatly.

Order your complete set today and start winning!